Confronted

By

The CROSS

Ministro Deborah Brewster

Favor & Blessings

By: Paul Wondracek

Published By
Paul Wondracek

ISBN-13: 978-1514389720

Printed in the United States of America

Acknowledgements

I would first like to thank The Holy Spirit for dropping this revelation in my spirit through His ever constant conversation and presence in my life. I would like to thank those in my life who helped make this book a reality. Thank you to my dear friend Bishop Jerry Grillo for your constant example of true Kingdom Leadership. Thank you to Pastor Daryl Miller for your graphic design expertise. Thank you to my wife Becky for putting up with my long hours and late nights completing this book after working and ministering all week. Thank you to Courtney Armstrong for your editing efforts and excitement over this project.

Table of Contents

Introduction

Do you find yourself frustrated because your evangelism efforts haven't produced much in your life? Many Christians today struggle with the most basic foundation of the Kingdom of God, the ministry of evangelism. Jesus' command to the church was *"Go into all the world and preach or proclaim the gospel to every creature, to every person."* So what does that look like? Most people aren't bold enough to tell others about the goodness of Jesus. Many individuals struggle with the confidence to be able to share their faith. This is a big problem in the Body of Christ. We've moved to being satisfied with church attendance rather than people truly being saved. Just because somebody goes to church doesn't mean that they're saved. We must understand this basic fundamental principal in the Kingdom of God.

Church is not the door into the Kingdom; Jesus is. Jesus says "I am the door." The only way into the Kingdom of God is through the door of the cross. I found myself frustrated as many other believers because we're trying to disciple people, teach them prosperity, teach them blessing, teach them about the Holy Spirit, teach them about the basic principles of the bible, the Christian faith and the Kingdom of God; however, we've skipped the most important step. The most important step is have they come through the door of the cross?

What would the greatest day on earth and the greatest moment in history be, if you could only pick just one moment? This is a profound question. Many think that the discovery that the earth was round would be one of the greatest moments in history, or the discovery of some particular law of physics, or some other great archeological find would be the greatest moment in history. Well, I believe the greatest moment in history was when the first drop of blood broke through the flesh of Jesus' body because that was the day the door of the kingdom was open forever and that was what led to the cross and the cross is the only way into the Kingdom of God.

I've titled this book *Confronted by the Cross* because everybody in their life will have to make a decision about the cross. **The cross is not a passive decision.** The cross is confrontational. The cross demands a decision and we're going to look at those two decisions and those choices in the coming pages of this book. When you come through the door of the cross you're introduced to pleasures forevermore in the Kingdom of God but we cannot skip the first and most important step. It's a relationship with God; it is understanding the confrontation of the cross.

Confronted by The Cross

So, how did this whole confronted by the cross thing start in my life anyway? Well, very recently I was having a conversation with God. I'm a marriage and family therapist as well as a bishop of a local church. I do marriage counseling and therapy for mental health patients, and I had just driven away from a session with a young, 17-year-old girl, who opened up to me about her substance abuse issues, the unhealthy treatment of her body, and her many immoral sexual relationships. As I was praying and talking to God in the car I said "Holy Spirit I want this person to be saved", and I started to think about all the good people in my life that were such good natured kind people, but didn't know Jesus, and I began to ask God how do I get these people saved. The Holy Spirit immediately corrected me and said, "It's not your job to get them saved son, your only job is to **confront them with the cross.**" This very phrase would prove to shift my ministry and make sharing the gospel of Jesus a very real part of my life. At that moment I asked another question because one of my mentors told me that questions are the most powerful success secret in life. **Answers hide from everything but the right question.**

We often ask God for petitions and ask God for **things** which are not wrong to do, but when the Bible says ask and it shall be given unto you, that doesn't necessarily mean just material things. **You can ask questions to God.** You can ask questions to the Holy Spirit, and He will answer you. I'm very conversational with God. I'm very conversational with the Holy Spirit and the more conversational I am, the quicker He responds. Having a conversation with God is one of the most powerful forms of asking that you'll ever do. So, back to my story. When I asked the Holy Spirit how do I help these people and share the gospel with them and get them saved, He told me it's not your job son to save them, it's not your job to get them saved, it's not your job to fix their life, your only job is to **confront them with the cross**. For the next 30 minutes, God started talking to me about what it means to confront somebody with the cross.

The cross is the greatest moment in history. The cross is not just a historical moment, the cross is a **door.** It is not only a door; it is THE DOOR to The Kingdom of God...the ONLY DOOR. Jesus said in scripture, 'I AM **THE** Way, The Truth, and The Life'. He didn't say I AM **a** way...He said 'I AM **THE WAY'**. The cross is the door into a new kingdom. The door into a new life. The door into a new eternity. Most people talk about the cross as if it is just some nice little story that Christians talk about or some historical folklore, but they never walk through the door of the cross to discover what's behind it. Jesus said I am the door, and many times we get saved, or we have a religious experience and we're done. We think that's it, but we don't understand **that the cross is an entry point into a world of tremendous pleasure, tremendous presence and tremendous purpose in your journey with God.**

The Holy Spirit continued to talk to me and he said these words. He said son when you confront people with the cross there are only two options or two responses once someone is confronted with the cross:

1.   They can either accept what Jesus did on the cross and receive everything that he provided through the cross. They can choose to believe and say yes to the cross, experience immediate transformation, immediate restoration in their relationship with God, and immediate access to heaven in eternity. Instantly they will receive everything that the cross provided for them.

2.   Or they can also choose to not believe. They can choose to not accept what Jesus did on the cross, and their life will continue on. They will continue to live life in a way that they see fit without God's involvement and without God's help, only to die and spend eternity in hell.

When you're confronted with the cross, these are the **only** two options you have; *to accept the cross or to not accept the cross.* Once you make that decision, **the consequences have already been set in motion,** either access to divine presence and eternal life or a life without God and eternity in hell. **The cross is confrontational.** The cross demands a decision. The cross is not inclusive. The cross is intensely individual and every person must be confronted with the cross. The final thing the Holy

Spirit said to me was that once you confront somebody with the cross and you invite them to either accept it or to not accept it; **their blood is no longer on your hands.** You don't have to fix them, you don't have to tell them any consequences, you don't have to change them; the blood is off of your hands because you've confronted them with the cross. Now it's the Holy Spirit's job to take it from there. Often times many Christians struggle with feeling like they have to be **Holy Spirit, Jr.** You don't have to be Holy Spirit, Jr. All you have to do is confront them with the cross. Once you do that, if they accept the cross the Holy Spirit will do the rest. They'll experience a born again moment when the Holy Spirit will make them aware of the forgiveness of their sins. The Holy Spirit will then infuse faith into their life and they'll be born again, **but THAT part is not your job.** The blood is off your hands.

You confronted them with the cross now you've got to let God be God and let the power of the cross begin to work in that person. **All you did was confront them and let them know the two choices that the cross demands.** Now it's up to you to understand that you obeyed God, you did what God told you to do, now God will do what He's marvelous at. God will do what He's magnificent at; that's changing a heart, forgiving our sins, and imparting to us his wisdom, his spirit and his power.

Seven Rewards for Obedience

1. ***Obedience brings the Favor of God****...favor is the reward for obedience. God is a reward God. He rewards those who obey Him it tells us in Hebrews 11:6.*

2. ***Obedience opens doors of access****...The Bible tells us that a man's gift makes room for him and brings him before great men. The word for gift is not talent but a man's seed or present opens up doors. When you obey the laws of God doors swing open wide.*

3. ***Obedience minimizes satan's hold on your life****...Ephesians 4 tells us that sin will give the devil a foothold. When we obey God's instructions to us, we no longer give the enemy a place to set up camp. We weaken his hold.*

4. ***Obedience protects those under your care****...The Bible is clear about sin being visited to the third and fourth generation in*

the book of Genesis. In order to protect your children and future generations, you must obey God. You're not only securing your own future but the future of those under your covering.

5. **Obedience builds trust between you and God**...*God is a heart God and we often talk about trusting God but few teach about God trusting us. The Bible talks about God entrusting talents to three men to see if He would get a return off of His investment. If God can trust you...He can elevate you! If you're faithful in little, He will make you ruler over much.*

6. **Obedience releases The Holy Spirit to begin doing His part of the work**...*Covenant means that you do your part and God will do His part; often God asks us to take the first action. When you do the natural God will do the super; your obedience releases Him to do His Part.*

7. **Obedience accelerates you to God's next instruction**...*God will never accelerate you past your last act of disobedience. You will*

never hear the next instruction from heaven if you did not obey the last one.

Too often in the church we try to get people closer to God, teach them about prayer, teach them about the bible, teach them about the Holy Spirit, but they haven't come through the door yet. They haven't gone to step one, which is to be confronted with the cross. **You cannot move to step three or step five if you've skipped step one.** Step three and five mean nothing until step one is taken. Step one is when you're confronted with the cross, which of the two decisions did you make? The consequences have already been decided. The rewards have already been created by God, but a decision has to be made. This profoundly changed my life. My car was, at that moment, so full of the presence of God as I sat in front of the gym that I was getting ready to go work out in, and just began to experience the joy of God's presence, as I realized God had just given me a mandate. God had just given me a mandate and an assignment, to confront people with the cross.

No longer would I try to increase church attendance, because there are churches all over the country full of people that don't believe the cross. Instantly I realized my only mandate was to confront them with the cross and invite them to make a choice. Wherever I preached, whoever I preached to this was my assignment. The cross demands a decision; either accept the cross and all Jesus did on it or don't. **The consequences have already been set in motion,** and the blood is no longer on my hands. The peace of God that instantly filled my heart and overwhelmed me is something that words on this page cannot describe. I began to look at everybody in my life that needed to be confronted by the cross.

Pray this prayer with me: Father forgive me for where I have tried to get people saved and do your job. I realize that my job is only to confront those around me with The Cross. I ask that you empower me to speak these words with confidence and grace and lead me to those that need to be confronted with The Cross daily.

Divine Interruption

Now an angel of the Lord said to Philip, "Go south to the road—the desert road—that goes down from Jerusalem to Gaza." [27] So he started out, and on his way he met an Ethiopian[a] eunuch, an important official in charge of all the treasury of the Kandake (which means "queen of the Ethiopians"). This man had gone to Jerusalem to worship, [28] and on his way home was sitting in his chariot reading the Book of Isaiah the prophet. [29] The Spirit told Philip, "Go to that chariot and stay near it."

[30] Then Philip ran up to the chariot and heard the man reading Isaiah the prophet. "Do you understand what you are reading?" Philip asked.

I thought about the scripture in Acts chapter 8 where Philip the evangelist saw an Ethiopian Eunuch in a chariot, and The Holy Spirit told Philip to join the Eunuch as he was reading the book of Isaiah, and I realized this is a perfect example of confronting someone with the Cross. In verse 37 of this passage, after Philip had preached Jesus and the Cross to him, the eunuch asked Philip, *"can I be baptized right now"*, and Philp answered him... *"Only If you believe with ALL of your heart"*. The eunuch answered him and said *"I believe that Jesus Christ is The Son of God."* Then Philip baptized him.

What is interesting about this passage is that Philip had to interrupt the eunuch who was in charge of all the treasury of the queen of Ethiopia. Philip had to risk being rejected as he confronted the eunuch while he was busy reading. Philip recognized a divine door, a moment where The Holy Spirit spoke to him and said confront this man with the cross. The eunuch just happened to be reading the Isaiah scroll. Philip didn't know that the eunuch was reading the Word, he just obeyed the voice of God, interrupting the man while he was reading. He used a real life situation to transition conversation to the cross. He didn't build relationship with the man or meet his physical need first. He simply confronted this eunuch with the Cross and let God do the rest.

Years later as the gospel spread throughout the world; when the Apostles reached Ethiopia, history tells us that they discovered hundreds of Churches already established. They realized that the Ethiopian Eunuch that Philip confronted on the side of the road and baptized, had taken the gospel to Ethiopia. Upon returning this Eunuch began to confront others with the Cross, and God began to grow the Church in his country before the Apostles even arrived there. That is the power of allowing someone to be confronted by the Cross. Philip confronted the eunuch with the cross and God began to work.

5 Keys to Power Evangelism

1. Recognize a God-moment...*Philip was able to recognize when the Holy Spirit was instructing him to confront the Eunuch. When confronting people with the cross you must look for a God opportunity in a conversation or a nudge from*

The Holy Spirit move the conversation in the direction of the cross.

2. Win their permission...*Before you confront them with the Cross ask for their perspective. Ask them what the Cross means to them or if they've ever heard of the Cross. Say things like..."What do you think?" This earns you your right to speak. If you've listened to them...they now will feel obligated to listen to you because you cared enough to get their perspective. Philip asked a questioned..."Do you understand what you're reading?"*

3. Present only the two Options...*don't go into theological details or ideas just present the two options either accept the cross or reject it and here are the results (discussed earlier in this chapter).*

4. Direct a decision...*Philip confronted the Eunuch until he decided to be baptized. Lead in with a question that will direct them to one of the only two choices. You can say things like "So have you accepted Him" or "would you like to accept what Jesus did now."*

5. Let the Holy Spirit work...*Realize that once you are finished confronting them with the Cross the blood is off your hands. You made them aware of the two choices and the results of either choice and now it's God's turn. Get out of the way and let God do what only He can ...Let the Holy Spirit draw and save. You're done with your job.*

In today's politically correct world of evangelism where we are taught to build relationship with the person or counsel them before we tell them about Jesus. The scripture is clear, nothing you do for a person matters in relation to their salvation **until they are confronted with the Cross and presented with the only two options.**

You may be asking well what if they want to think about it. Well they can; but at that moment they are aware of the only two options. Thinking about it means that they have chosen option two, not accepting the Cross at the present moment. They are not guaranteed that The Holy Spirit will draw them again to the cross. The Bible is clear when it says, no one comes to The Father unless the Holy Spirit draws them. One cannot get saved at any time but only when confronted by the cross. The Holy Spirit then begins to work and that window of time demands either acceptance of the Cross or not.

Remember Jesus said "You didn't chose me...but I chose you." In other words, the decision is yours to accept but God definitely made the first move 2000 years ago when He hung on an old rugged cross for you and me. He chose you with that act of selfless love and sacrifice. Just because He chose you doesn't mean that you will choose to accept that. Many that God has chosen are in hell today because they did not choose Him by accepting what He did on the cross. Jesus died for the world but that only created the potential for all to be saved and opened the DOOR to The Kingdom. There is a second part to John 3:16 we forget to read. *"That whosoever believes in Him should not perish but have eternal life."* Many preachers are preaching the *"For God so loved the world that He gave His only begotten son"*, and telling people that God loves all people and all people will be saved. That is a lie...the second part of the verse proves this. *"That whosoever believes in Him will not parish but have everlasting LIFE."* Only those who BELIEVE IN HIM shall benefit from the cross. The cross demands a decision. God is not asking us what we think about it...it's not up for debate. It is simply an invitation that demands an RSVP.

There are people in your life you may feel will be offended when you confront them with the cross, and you fear losing the relationship.

Confronting someone with the cross does not mean that you judge them or write them off if they do not accept what Jesus did. If you confront them with the cross over conversation one day and simply ask the question; have you accepted what Jesus did and do you believe it with your heart? They may say no, and if they do you just simply continue the conversation or move on to something else because you did your job. We don't shove the gospel down people's throat and be rude. Confronting them does not mean yelling or being pushy. It simply means letting them know the only two options, asking them if they have accepted, and also if they would like to. If they do not accept option 1 then change the subject and let The Holy Spirit begin His work. Your relationship with that person does not change; you just keep loving them and praying for them and let God do what He does best.

Whoever Looks

Jesus said something very profound in the gospels. He said *"As Moses was lifted up in the wilderness so shall the Son of man be lifted up."* (John 3:14). What Jesus was referring to was the Old Testament passage in the Bible where God judged the Israelites in the wilderness for their idolatry when snakes came out of the earth and began to bite the people. Moses was instructed by God to form a serpent out of gold and place it on a pole, and everyone who looked at that snake would LIVE and be healed instantly and they were. Translation: Jesus was saying that **society had been snake bit.** Just like the Israelites in the wilderness and the golden serpent that Moses fashioned; the Son of God would be placed on a pole called the Cross, and lifted up.

Now why would Jesus compare Himself to a snake on a pole? Well, it's very simple, but profound. A snake represents the CURSE or SIN...and the Bible tells us that Jesus, the one who knew no sin, BECAME sin for us...that we might become the righteousness of God in Christ Jesus. Jesus became SIN on the cross that is why The Father could not look at Him and turn His back. Jesus didn't just take your sin...He became sin. He became the serpent...He became the curse. Just like Moses' golden serpent on the pole, Jesus became SIN on a tree called the Cross. Whoever looked at that golden serpent lived, and whoever looks at Jesus on the cross shall LIVE. Why did I tell you this? Simple because ALL the hard work was already done. Your job is just to tell people to LOOK and LIVE! Your job is just to tell people the direction to look and let them gaze upon the crimson stained body of The Son of God for a moment and if they accept that sacrifice they will LIVE! Just confront them with the cross and God will do the rest.

Pray this prayer with me...Father in Jesus Name I ask that you would empower me with Your Spirit to reach out to others with the Gospel today. Help me to see Divine Opportunities today and be sensitive to the leading of The Holy Spirit as You give me the Power to confront people with The Cross. In Jesus Name...Amen!

Decisions, Decisions

You cannot make disciples until you encourage decisions. Believing is a decision and **decisions decide EVERYTHING.** The Cross demands a decision because there are only two options. There are no maybes or I'll think about it. God is a vastly complicated being who makes things very simple in order for us to access His greatness. In the beginning the tree in the Garden of Eden required a decision and the tree on Golgotha required a decision as well. Life and death come down to a decision over a tree called the CROSS.

That's how it was in the very beginning and that is how it is now. It is so important to stress the decision part of The Cross. Faith is a decision that is motivated by an encounter with Jesus that The Holy Spirit gives you after you have been confronted by the cross. Here is what most people don't understand...not making a decision IS a decision. It is a decision to NOT participate in something.

The Law of Exchange

The Cross is simply an exchange. Jesus became what you were so that you could become what He is. He became a curse so that you could become blessed. He became sin so that you could become righteousness. He became sickness so that you could be healed. The Bible even says that He became poor in II Corinthians 8:9 so that for His sake you might become RICH!! **The Cross is a wealth exchange.** God is taking everything bad in your life and giving you everything good that He has. Let me use the analogy of a tree in real life. Humans inhale oxygen and exhale carbon dioxide, but trees take in the carbon dioxide that we breathe out and give off oxygen. It's like one needs the other to live. If it weren't for trees giving off oxygen as a byproduct, we as humans would not have the oxygen we need to live. Well that's how The Cross works... The Cross takes in your sin, curse and shame, and the cross releases back to you life, healing, and forgiveness. What an awesome analogy. The Cross and Jesus' death on it was a great exchange and if you're willing to exhale your sins and let Jesus take them... The Cross is ready to release all of God's Blessing and Favor right back to YOU!!!

The Church Today

I'm so concerned as I watch the Church today in all of its growth and multiplication around the world and especially in America. We are seeing large growing Churches move away from talking about and preaching on foundational issues such as the Cross, Sin and the consequences for sin. There is no salvation without conviction of sin. That's like going to the doctor and having him write you a prescription without even diagnosing you. It is impossible to effectively bring a solution to an issue unless you first correctly identify the problem. A solution will do you no good unless you're first willing to identify the problem. Most people are pretending not to see their issue but they need to know that the Cross is a SOLUTION to a huge problem called SIN.

10 Things that water down the Gospel:

- Lack of training waters down the Gospel…
- Not teaching God's expectations for living His way…
- Remaining silent about the sin issues currently affecting society…
- Lack of prayer waters down the Gospel…
- Lack of persistence waters down the Gospel…
- Only talking about the blessing side of God and not the judgment side of God…
- Lack of mentorship and accountability – the lone ranger spirit…
- Staying behind the four walls of the Church only and not being a light in the world, on our jobs and in our communities…
- Not walking in love and forgiving those who offend us…
- Poor Church attendance and priority on the things of God…

Trending Churches love to talk about what The Cross provides and all the blessings of God that The Cross brings with it, however, we have a problem in the Church. We have Churches full of members who live lifestyles unapproved by God.

The Cross doesn't just affect your future, it changes how you live RIGHT NOW!!! The Cross didn't just make you righteous but it also has given you the power to continue to walk in a way that pleases God. **Love has expectations; Divine Love has Divine Expectations.** Wisdom is the ability to discern right and wrong; right and wrong has been clearly laid out for us by God in His Word. The problem in the Church is that many people who think they are saved are really not because they were not properly confronted with the Cross. They were told that Church membership saved them or because they're daddy was a Christian they are now saved. None of those things are true. Because we haven't properly confronted people with the Cross we haven't truly given them the opportunity to understand what being saved really means. If you confront people with the Cross correctly in the beginning, then they are more likely to understand what they were saved and delivered from, as well as what they are delivered to.

Out and In

Many Churches don't understand the two sides of the Cross. The part of the Cross that brought you OUT…and the part of the Cross that brings you IN. Moses helped the Israelites come

OUT of the slavery of Egypt, but Joshua helped bring Israel INTO the Promised Land; these are two very different things. Many Christians have been saved OUT of but not INTO. They were delivered out of sin and destructive lifestyles, but have failed to allow the Cross to take them INTO the Blessing and Favor of God. Here is the problem…many other so-called Christians were delivered into the Blessings of God and His favor through the Cross BUT they never came OUT of their lifestyles. They were saved INTO but not OUT OF, and unless you've been saved OUT OF sin, bondage, and destructive behaviors…you cannot be saved or delivered INTO prosperity, blessing, and the favor of God. So their conversions were not genuine. **You've got to come out before you can go in, and many in the Church are trying to go IN and they've never allowed the Cross to bring them OUT.** Therefore we have a lot of saints that are AINT'S. This is a powerful principle to understand that there are two sides to the Cross and you cannot walk in the Blessings of the Kingdom until you get delivered from the bondage of SIN. You've got to let the Cross bring you OUT before it can bring you IN.

Pray this Prayer with me: Father I come to you making a decision to accept the cross and give you my sins. Bring me out of bondage and sin and take me into your favor and blessing by The Cross of Jesus. I pray that you would empower me to preach the Cross and confront people with the importance of making a decision. Do your work through me in Jesus Name, Amen!

Not a way...THE WAY

There is much debate in the Church today and in our country about Christianity and Jesus, and there being many ways to God. Oprah and Yanla and other self-help gurus are all of a sudden making themselves experts on Christian theology; trying to indicate that Jesus is not the ONLY way to heaven. This is very dangerous and deceptive. **Fame does not qualify you to speak for God or establish**

Christian Doctrine. The calling of God and the delegated Authority of the Church does however qualify one to speak. The commissioning as Apostles' and Bishops' in the Church qualifies them to establish doctrine and interpret scripture correctly and this is accomplished though much mentorship and training, not fame.

The Church is allowing personalities and famous celebrities to have a platform and speak about things that they know nothing about. Let's look at what Jesus Himself said in John 14:6 where He stated… *"I Am the way, the truth, and the life."* Now this is very interesting to me that Jesus never said I am **A** way…if you read the same Bible that I read; He said I Am **THE** way. There is a huge difference in those two terms and we need to look at it for the sake of the Church, so that you will preach the gospel properly; that when God gives you opportunity you won't blow it like so many people have and so often do. There are not many ways to God folks. The New Testament is very clear about Jesus being the ONLY way to The Father.

Jesus Himself specified that, as we just read earlier. When you confront people with the Cross, they need to understand that Jesus is not one option to God or heaven, but that He is the ONLY option.

The rest of the verse we just read is very clear as Jesus continues to say... *"No man comes to the Father except through ME."* (John 14:6). Well there is even more clarification by Jesus Christ Himself that you CANNOT come to or have access to The Father (GOD) except through JESUS. He even went a step further regarding being the only way to God, but also that He was and IS God. He is the third person in the Godhead or the Trinity. He said before Abraham was I AM when talking to the Pharisees indicating that He is the I AM that spoke to Moses out of the burning bush.

Why is this so important? **You can't preach what you don't know and you can't lead where you won't go.** The Cross is so important because it is not just one of many ways. The Cross is the ONLY way! We need to make sure we have that in mind as a part of the foundation of our Christian life and understanding. I remember being on a radio program talking about my book on the Blood of Jesus and on that particular program I was asked by the host whether or not I thought Jesus was the only way. I remember answering very clearly that Jesus stated I Am THE way not A way. Well the radio host did not appear to like that too much so he proceeded to take calls and open up the phone lines. Muslims and Buddhists and other religious people began to call in and berate me about how wrong I was. So this huge debate began about is Jesus the only way. **Folks the Cross is confrontational.** When you really preach the Cross of Jesus there is no grey area...He is the ONLY way to the Father. He is the only way to heaven.

Now that program got really chaotic really fast and the host finally hung up on me. I never raised my voice or got angry; I just spoke the truth and preached the TRUE Gospel and confronted them with the Cross. The reason the trendy Church is not preaching the True Gospel is because it invites persecution. When you say that Jesus is THE way and everyone else is wrong your mailing list begins to shrink and the invites stop coming, WHY? Because the cross is confrontational. **You don't have a right to preach it in the popular way; its God's story not yours and you must preach the TRUTH.** This Gospel wasn't your idea or my idea. It has to be ministered with integrity to the true intention of God Himself.

Seven Keys for recognizing a true Voice for God:

1. A true Voice for God has a history of training and preparation in the things of God...

2. A true Voice for God doesn't trade power for popularity...and will tell the truth of God's Word even if it means being ridiculed...

3. A true Voice for God will never deny Jesus as the only Way to the Father and to Heaven...

4. A true Voice for God will be surrounded by quality mentors and submit to Kingdom Authority...they will be in authority and under authority...

5. A true Voice for God will never seek the destruction of another person...

6. A true Voice for God will never put culture above Kingdom...

7. A True Voice for God will be transparent about their own shortcomings and failures so others can learn from them...

The goal is not to get into an argument, but if it comes up it has to be clarified. You need to understand that in your own Christian walk so that you are not deceived. Jesus is THE way and there is no other way but HIM.

Pray this Prayer with me: Father in Jesus Name allow me to preach the true Gospel that you are THE Way not a way, but the only way to the Father. Please allow me to confront people with the cross and not give in to the deception of the popular opinions of the day but to stand on The Word of God and preach on Jesus Christ as the WAY to heaven in Jesus Name, Amen!

Access has a Price

The Cross was the price for access. Access always has a price; the price to have access to God was the blood of His Son on The Cross. Not everybody can access the Throne of heaven. That access to an appointment with the Father had a price. God's price was perfection and only perfect people could enter that is why no one has ever seen God. So He provided the payment Himself and granted access through The Cross. The Cross is the payment for access to The Father. No one can have access to Him any other way. Access has a price and faith is the currency…faith in The Son of God through the Cross.

To have a meeting with Donald Trump you have to know someone who knows him. To have a meeting with the president you have to be invited. **To have a meeting with God you have to know someone who knows Him**…His Son Jesus. If you come through Him the requirement for access is met. He said NO MAN can come to the Father except through ME.

If you will understand this principle about access, you will understand the Cross. In the Garden of Eden, access to God was open to all. Once Adam sinned and disobeyed God by eating of the fruit he was commanded not to eat from, access was cut off. God has a protocol and sin is not allowed in His presence. You cannot just walk up into a fortune 500 company and go to the CEO's office and sit down for coffee with the CEO. You need and appointment. You cannot just go to a concert of a world famous band and go back stage whenever you feel like it. Access is exclusive!!! So why do people think that you can just walk up into God's presence. He is greater than anyone I just mentioned.

He is The KING. In a monarchy no one could have access to the King unless the King summoned them. If a meeting was requested, the King has to give them an opportunity. If the guest came into the King's chamber without an invitation, he could be killed. We in America do not understand Monarchies. Kings are held in such high honor that no one came in without an appointment. Yet, we as Christians think that we can come to God whenever we want. Well we can, but there is a price.

Your Way Has Been Paid

The price for access to the King of Kings is blood. That's right we lost access to the Father when Adam sinned and only blood will take care of the price of access. God paid your way. God gave His own Son as the payment of access again. The only way one can enter God's presence is to be perfect and spotless. The only way for fallen humanity to enter the presence of God is through the blood of Jesus. Jesus paid for your access to the Father. **The price was His blood on the Cross.** Your faith accesses the Blood and the Blood gives you access to The Father. So the next time you toss up a little prayer, remember the price that was paid for that prayer to reach the ears of The Father. God wanted you in His presence so bad that He sacrificed His own Son to give you access. Have you taken that access for granted?

In the Old Testament only the High Priest had access to God's presence once a year. There was only one person who could enter the presence of God or the Holy of Holies and that was the High Priest. If there was any sin in the High Priest's life or if he came into God's presence in the wrong protocol, the angel of The Lord would kill him right in the Holy of Holies. The book of Leviticus tells us that bells were placed on the High Priest's robe, and a rope wrapped around his ankle so that if iniquity was found in him and he dropped dead in the Holy of Holies the other priests would hear it and pull his body out. That is how serious access to the presence of God is. Prayer is all about ACCESS!

5 Keys to Effective Prayer

1. *Take access by the Blood of Jesus very seriously.* Believe that your prayers make a difference.

2. *Enter God's presence with a song and with thanksgiving.* Understand that you are talking

to The King and there was a price for your appointment.

3. *Be conversational with God* not religious sounding. Jesus said God does not hear you because of your many words.

4. *Speak words from your heart* not words to try to impress God. Let Him know how you really feel about Him.

5. *Have a place set aside in your home* just for talking to God every morning. IT'S called your secret place.

Access has a price, never forget that. Let's talk about the price for access in every area of your life. What is the price for access to your future? Simple, your present is the price for your future. **What you do today determines what you experience tomorrow.** It's called the law of the seed. Today is either a harvest from your past or a seed for your future. **In order to get into your future you must master today and invest in your tomorrow.** This generation is failing miserably because someone lied to them and told them to spend their today instead of INVEST in their today. There are two things that you can do with time...spend it or INVEST it. Time is the only thing that God is not making any more of. What you do with time and access is what determines your success in life.

The cross is all about TIME and ACCESS. The Cross was an intersection of two types of time...Chronos time and Kairos time. Horizontal or linear time and vertical time or God's time. Chronos time is a linear time that we use to determine days and hours and minutes. That is where we get the word chronological. Kairos time is seasons or moments. God operates off of Kairos time which is appointed times and seasons. The Cross is where both time and destiny intersected. Human time and Heavenly time intersected at the Cross. **It is the place where God and man reconnected and came into proper alignment again.** God and man were once again back in step with each other just like Adam was in the Garden of Eden.

There are only two things that you can do with your time. Spend it or INVEST it. When you spend it it's gone...when you invest it...it returns to you as your FUTURE! Time and access are the two most important things in your life and both must be used to connect with God. What will you do with your time and access? Will you squander it like most people, or will you recognize its VALUE and understand its benefits?

The secret to succeeding in life is to learn how to have a successful day. Because a life is a day repeated over and over. Those who have terrible lives have continued to experience terrible days. They have not learned the art of creating a perfect day. If you know how to create a perfect day you will create the perfect life. Always start your day in divine presence; start your day in your secret place. You don't have to pray long just let God be your first conversation. Genesis 1 tells us in the beginning was GOD. Every beginning must have God in it if it is going to be successful. If you start your day with a God conversation or a God moment; it will start off right. The art of time management is one of the most popular subjects on bookstore shelves today; yet nothing is mentioned about starting your day with God.

There is a secret to creating the perfect day and I want to share it with you. Remember the secret to access your future is your present. So what you do in your present determines your future. There are twelve keys to a perfect day.

12 Keys to Managing a Day:

1. *Preparation*...prepare for the next day the night before. Always write down your tasks and appointments the night before. When you start your day you won't waste time gathering your tasks but you have them ready from the night before.

2. *Meditation*...spend some time in thought everyday meditating on the Word of God. Every day should have a time to savor moments and reflect on what made you feel good the day before.

3. *Motivation*...protect your passion. Passion is not something you can create, it is something you can only protect. Protect your motivation by limiting the distractions that you give attention too. True goals motivate you and placing your written goals in front of you create motivation.

4. *Organization*...order is crucial to success. Order is the accurate arrangement of things. Order is sequential and tasks should be placed in

order of importance and priority. Take a small step towards order every day. Use the E.H.A.H. method for organizing. Everything Has A Home. Everything in your life should have a place or a home so that you don't have to go looking for it every time.

5. *Elimination*…what you decide not to do is just as important as what you decide to do. If our body do not eliminate than our health becomes jeopardized. Decide what you will not give attention to today! Take your future back one "NO" at a time.

6. *Delegation*…Never do what another can do better than you. The secret to multiplying your impact is to delegate tasks to the people in your life that are most gifted to complete them. Stick to what you're good at and delegate the things you're not good at to others.

7. *Impartation*…I love this word…it means to share without losing what you have. To impart to another is what life is all about. Everyday should include a moment where you impart your joy, knowledge, peace, wisdom, or life experience into another's life. It should also

include others being able to impart into your life as well.

8. *Inspiration*…The secret to success is not to try and inspire yourself or to wait for God to inspire you. The secret to success is to FIND what inspires you and place it in front of you. What pictures or people inspire you? Find them and stay near them because keeping yourself inspired is the key to a successful day and a successful life.

9. *Information*…If you are not a learner today is the best you'll ever be. If you're not a learner then your present has just become your future. Learning is the key to leading. Learn something every day. Seek out mentorship and ask questions…it will create incredible amounts of energy in your life.

10. *Celebration*…every day you should celebrate small victories. Celebration is so important in your daily life. How do you celebrate? Reward yourself daily for completed tasks or projects. Maybe you like a specific meal or a game of golf. See these as rewards for accomplished goals.

11. *Documentation...*Dignify your discoveries by writing them down. Every day should include some type of journaling or documentation of what you learned and what inspired you. Journal about what made you feel good that day. Develop a wisdom journal to write down what you learn from your mentors.

12. *Restoration...*at the end of every day you need to restore yourself by learning to rest properly and take care of your body. Get enough sleep at night and make getting ready to sleep a spa like experience. Even God rested on the seventh day so obviously rest is as important as work. Have a time everyday where you unwind and savor quiet peaceful moments with the ones you love. The law of diminishing returns states that the more work you do without rest the less productive you become. Rest multiplies your effectiveness.

Hurry is your Enemy

That is one of the most profound things that I ever learned about managing a day. The list above will help you to experience all that the Cross has purchased for you. You will be a master of TIME and ACCESS in your everyday life. There is another thing that God showed me one day about managing your time. We live in a very fast paced society and most of us feel hurried from task to task. **Hurry is the enemy of order.** Hastiness is something that will rob you of moments and keep you from savoring every day and investing the time God has given you effectively. God does not do anything FAST. He has been preparing supper for 4000 years; He unfolds the purpose of His will over generations. We, however, rush through moments and miss the pleasure of a conversation or a task because we live a hurried life and don't know how to master TIME and ACCESS. This is a method God showed me one day. One morning my mind was racing and my thoughts were going a mile a minute; I was extremely stressed out by my work load, life issues, and stresses. My phone was ringing off the hook and text messages were dinging left and right. I couldn't take it anymore I just shut my phones off and went to bed and put the pillow over my head to just shut the world OUT!

As I laid there The Holy Spirit began to speak to me about something called being in bondage to the urgent. Everything is vying for your attention. Everything is competing to distract you and demand you pay attention to it. It can be the urgency to answer your phone, your text, and your social media notifications. Smart phones have multiplied this problem exponentially and have caused us to be in bondage to the urgent. We find ourselves rushing through our day and letting everyone else control our every moment; demanding a response from us. God spoke to me and said "Do not be in bondage to the urgent." Do not allow the urgent demand for your attention to move you to respond. It's not a race! Learn to slow down and gather yourself. Learn to move purposefully and methodically through your day. **Slow down until excellence becomes easy.**

Pray this prayer with me: Father thank you for access and time, the two greatest gifts that The Cross provided to me. Help me to use these gifts to glorify Your Name on a daily basis. In Jesus Name...Amen!

A System for Success

Now that we have explored the method of confronting people with the Cross, let's recap the first few chapters into a practical guide to make it easy for you to apply these truths to your daily life. I have outlined a 7 step process to effectively confront people with the Cross. These seven keys will make it easy

If you want to be effective at communicating the Gospel of Jesus, there are a few pillars that are unchanging that you must follow through on. These were explained in deeper detail in the first two chapters, however, I am getting ready to package that information into a simple system or check list.

How to confront someone with The Cross:

o The GOD-MOMENT - during conversation with an individual...look for the GOD-MOMENT. The moment when The Holy Spirit nudges you or the window opens that you feel in your heart is a good time to Segway into the conversation. This step is crucial because God may already be drawing that person by His Spirit and the timing on your words will confirm what God has already been speaking to them. *Philip was able to recognize when the Holy Spirit was instructing him to confront the Eunuch. When confronting people with the cross you must look for a God opportunity in a conversation or a nudge from The Holy Spirit to move the conversation in the direction of the cross.*

o PERMISSION – always Segway with a question. When confronting them with the cross solicit their opinion about God. Ask them what they think about The Cross or the Bible. This step will create permission. Once you listen to their thoughts on the Cross immediately in their mind you create permission to speak to them. This is the law of listening. *Philip asked a questioned...”Do you understand what you're reading?”*

o CONFRONT THEM WITH THE CROSS – now this is your time to shine. Tell them about the Cross and the free gift of forgiveness and salvation. Tell them about the perfect sacrifice of Jesus and how God so loved the world that He gave us His Son. Talk about how the Cross changed your life and how the burden of your sins were lifted. Remind them that the cross is the greatest moment in history. The cross is not just a historical moment, the cross is a door. It is not a door only, it is THE DOOR to The Kingdom of God...the ONLY DOOR. Jesus said in scripture I AM THE Way, The Truth, and The Life. He didn't say I AM a way...He said I AM THE WAY. The cross is the door into a new kingdom. The Cross is the place of exchange...your sin for His righteousness, your curse for His Blessing, your shame for His Peace.

o TWO OPTIONS – this is where you share there are only two options. 1. They can accept what Jesus did on the cross and receive everything that he provided through the cross. They can choose to believe and say yes to the cross, and experience **immediate** transformation, immediate restoration in their relationship with God, and immediate access to heaven in eternity. Instantly they will receive everything that the cross provided for them.

2. They can also choose to not believe. They can choose to not accept what Jesus did on the cross, and their life will continue on and they will continue to live life in a way that they see fit without God's involvement and without God's help, only to die and spend eternity in hell. When you're confronted with the cross, those are the only two options you have; to accept the cross or to not accept the cross. Once you make that decision, the consequences have already been set in motion, either access to divine presence and eternal life or a life without God and eternity in hell. *Don't go into theological details or ideas, just present the two options – either accept the cross or reject it and here are the results.*

- o DIRECT a decision - The Cross DEMANDS a response...*Philip confronted the Eunuch until he decided to be baptized. Lead in with a question that will direct them to one of the only two choices. You can say things like "So have you accepted Him" or "would you like to accept what Jesus did now."*

- o Let the Holy Spirit work...*Realize that once you are finished confronting them with the Cross, the blood is off your hands. You made them aware of the two choices and the results of either choice, now its God's turn. Get out of the way and let God do what only He can ...Let the Holy Spirit draw and save. You're done with your job.* Let it go…let them go and continue on as if you never did anything. You are not Holy Spirit junior. You don't need to help God out. Jesus saves…we do not. Know at this point that you have obeyed the mandate of heaven that Jesus gave. You have fulfilled the great commission and confronted someone with The Cross. Great job! Now watch God work!

You now know how to lead someone to Jesus. It is really that easy. You don't have to get them to an alter or make them choose all you have to do is

Confront them with The Cross. So let's make it even easier and simpler to follow these seven steps:

1. God-moment
2. Permission
3. Confront
4. Two options
5. Direct a decision
6. Let God do His job
7. Pray for them

These seven easy steps make sharing your faith an everyday event. There is so much great revelation in this book and I have a lot more to say about The Cross, but if you walk away not knowing how to practically share your faith then this book is a failure. I felt the need to create a system of evangelism according to the scriptures that would make telling others about Christ an easy and rewarding experience. This is not some gimmick that I just came up with. This teaching came out of a true encounter with The Holy Spirit. Once you understand the system, it is like a weight falls off of your shoulders. **The burden of saving people is not yours to carry.** Jesus is the only One that can save! Now you can rest and know that confronting others with the Cross is simple and you are now aware of God's expectations for you.

Savior to Lord

Now there is a real dilemma in the body of Christ. All that we just learned about confronting people with the Cross is about receiving Jesus as Savior. Accepting the free gift of salvation is the main purpose of the Cross. This is only the beginning. We've talked about coming through the cross, and how the Cross of Jesus is the door into the Kingdom. That is true, but it doesn't end there and unfortunately many Christians stop their journey right there; when Jesus took it a step further. There are two sides to the Cross. One side receives Him as Savior but the other side of the Cross submits to Him as Lord. The Church has failed to move from seeing Him as savior to receiving Him as KING.

Jesus being your Savior came THROUGH the Cross...but Jesus being your LORD only comes through your CARRYING your Cross. You must carry the Cross in order to make Him Lord of your life. What does that mean? What does carrying a cross signify? Carrying a Cross signifies that soon you will DIE. Most of us cannot receive Jesus as Lord because we have not died to our own desires, hatred and plans. Carrying your cross means that you are willing to submit to His instructions and drop your agenda for your life.

Don't call Him LORD…if he doesn't govern your decisions. Don't call Him LORD…if anything goes. Don't call Him LORD…if you cannot submit to someone you can see (Mentors and Leaders). Don't call Him LORD…if He doesn't have your money. Then He is your Savior which is fine. Jesus being your savior means you got through the door. Making Jesus your LORD means that you will find out what's behind the door.

You cannot have a resurrection until you have a death. So many in the body of Christ want to walk in resurrection POWER! But in order to have a resurrection you have to DIE. Most people don't like the dying part. Now I don't mean physical death…I mean you have to die to your own wants and desires so you can please your King. The Apostle Paul made it clear in Galatians 2:20 when he said *"I am crucified with Christ, it is no longer I who live…but Christ who lives in me and the life I now live I live by faith in the Son of God who loved me and gave Himself for me."* Apostle Paul new the secret to living was dying.

Dying to your doubts…

Dying to your desires…

Dying to your decisions…

Dying to your demands…

Once you die…understand that now you qualify for resurrection. You will be raised in faith…raised in His desires…raised in His decisions and raised in His demands. He took you from a sinner and made you a saint…but God is trying to get you to understand that you are now a son.

Counterfeit Witnesses

We've heard the term thrown around many times "We are witnesses". Many traditional churches have a witnessing ministry that goes door to door telling people about Jesus. This is a noble pursuit, however, a witness is more than just someone who throws a few scriptures at people and prays a prayer. Yes, it is true that we are called to be witnesses, so what is a witness? Witnesses are usually called into court to testify as to what they saw and heard that relates to the events of the case. A witness is never someone who just tells a story. A counterfeit witness is someone who tells a story about something that they were witness to, but never really EXPERIENCED. The Church is full of counterfeit witnesses; that are telling the story of Jesus without ever really experiencing the PERSON of Jesus. The scriptures tell us in the book of Acts, that during Peter's sermon he stated this phrase: *"We cannot help but speak of that which we have seen and heard"*. (Acts 4:20). What's my point? You're not qualified to be a witness, until you have seen something, heard something, or experienced something. You will never be an effective witness for Jesus until you have seen Him by Faith, heard His Words, and experienced His touch in your life. You can't teach what you don't know, and you can't lead where you won't go.

You must share the message of Jesus from a deep seated experience with Him. One of my favorite scriptures is found in the book of Acts Chapter 4 and verse 14 when those who were flogging the disciples for preaching said this; *"When they saw the boldness of Peter and John, and realized that they were uneducated ordinary men, they realized that they had been with Jesus"*. That's the KEY! They had been with Jesus. It's only when you have been with Jesus that He touches your life with the power to be a WITNESS. You can now speak of that which you have seen and heard, that the Cross is the door into the Kingdom of God. Spending time with the Master makes talking about Him so much easier.

If I am trying to describe my wife to another person, but have never spent much time with her; I will not be an effective witness for her. I would probably throw out some details about her age and hair color. However, when I have spent significant time with her and learned her likes and dislikes, I now become a witness to who she really is. I'll be able to tell someone how kind and compassionate she is, as well as be able to describe her character and qualities. It's the same with Jesus. The more you get to know Him, the easier it will be to discuss Him with others and share about the wonder He is.

12 proofs that God is working in your life

1. When you do wrong you are convicted...
2. There is opposition to your vision and goals...
3. You have a hunger for God's Word...
4. You practice the Presence of God daily...
5. You feel compassion for others to be whole...
6. You desire to take your family to Church...
7. You seek out mentorship easily...
8. You have a sense of calling on your life...
9. People with need are attracted to you...
10. You have a hunger for excellence...
11. Your appetite for sin decreases...
12. You begin to think about your future frequently...

Pray this prayer with me:

Father I come to you in the name of Jesus and I thank you that I have accepted what you did on the Cross and I'm so grateful for your grace. I not only have accepted you as savior but I also receive you as Lord...as my King. I die to my own desires and demands and I pick up yours. Use me to confront others with the Cross and see many receive the same grace and favor that I am walking in. In Jesus Name Amen!

Seven Sentences from
The Cross

In these finals chapters I thought it would be important to focus on something that is often overlooked by people.   Last words are very important in the Bible. In the book of Malachi the last book of the Old Testament, God said some pretty important things to the Priests and the nation prior to not speaking again for 400 years. In Acts chapter one right before Jesus ascended to the Father He said…Go to Jerusalem and *"wait for the Gift of My Father…"* (Acts 1:4). He was speaking of the coming of the Holy Spirit. **So last words matter and should be looked at carefully because there is usually a message in them.** Jesus spoke seven phrases on the cross right before He died and then rose again three days later. Let's look at each phrase and see why they were so important for you and me today:

1.   "Father forgive them…for they know not what they do".

While He was dying for you…He was praying for you!

Forgiveness is the primary reason for the cross. Jesus gave us an example of true forgiveness. Most of us forgive when someone says "I'm sorry". That is not forgiveness…that is an accepted apology. Forgiveness occurred while the blood was still running down Jesus' arms. **Can you forgive when you're still bleeding?** When the wound is still fresh. Forgiveness is the most powerful weapon on earth. It disarms satan. Forgiving someone means, not wanting them to pay anymore. You see Jesus is teaching us the importance of forgiveness. No marriage will last without FORGIVENESS. We are flawed people and many of the blessings God has for us are held up, because we refuse to forgive. Unforgiveness damages you more than it does the person who hurt you. It is giving the person who hurt you power over your life. Unforgiveness is like drinking poison while expecting the other person to die. Not going to happen; the only one you're killing is you. Jesus not only forgave us, but also said... *"Father forgive them"*. Many times we just want God to get them back. Get em God! Well, if you've truly forgiven them, you may also pray like Jesus did, *"Father forgive them"*. Pray for the grace of God to cover those who hurt you. God's judgment is a whole lot worse than yours, so ask God to forgive them too!

2.   "Today you will be with me in Paradise" (Luke 23:43). Paradise is not heaven, paradise was the waiting place that all Old Testament saints went to after death, like David and Abraham. That's right, Jesus had not risen yet so none of them could go to heaven. Jesus had to go to paradise first and redeem the saints of old. Matthew 27:52 says that after Jesus died the rocks split open and many Holy People came out of their tombs and walked around the city. Jesus went and got them out of paradise.

If the waiting place was called paradise, heaven must be amazing. **Before He got us...He had to get them!** He got you so He could get them. Jesus didn't just save you for you. He had many people in mind when He saved you. When God saved Billy Graham He had millions in mind. **God is never just talking to one person.** When He talked to Adam He was talking to Humanity, when He talked to Abraham He was talking to a Nation, and when He talked to the twelve disciples He was talking to the Church. When God speaks to you He is speaking to everything and everyone connected to YOU!

3. **"Father into your hands I commit my Spirit" (Luke 23:46).** When Jesus said these words the Curtain of the Temple was torn from top to bottom. What Jesus was saying was simple...He was saying this is the LAST day God dwells in a building! God would no longer live in a temple, but now He would live in His people. That's right...the Holy Spirit left the temple when Jesus uttered those words and then filled God's people in Acts chapter one. God was no longer dwelling in a building made with man's hands...but in US. The Church is not a building, the Church is a people. The Bible calls us LIVING STONES in I Peter 2:5. The Church is now the Body of Christ, the people of

God. Jesus was saying, now the Kingdom that was WITH them…will be IN them. The Kingdom of God is now living inside of you. **Jesus gave up His Spirit so you could receive His Spirit.** The Bible tells us in Colossians 1:27 *"Christ in you, the hope of Gory"*. The Glory of God is not in a building anymore, now the Glory of God is in His people; you and me!

4. **"My God My God, why have you forsaken me" (Matthew 27:46).** This is the only time in the New Testament where Jesus addressed His Father as GOD. Jesus always addressed God as Father, because of His relationship to the Father. But on the cross, Jesus became like US; distant from The Father and forsaken. Remember, He took our place. So He cried out My God! On the cross is the only time Jesus ever knew the Father from a distance, calling Him God. Normally, people call Him God because they don't know Him personally as the Father. **But Jesus called Him God…so you could call Him FATHER.** Jesus knew Him from a distance on the cross…so you could know Him up close as your Father in heaven. Hallelujah!

5.   "Mother here is your son" (John 19:26).
Jesus is the Word of God so He obeyed the Word of God to a tee. Jesus made sure He took care of His Family, even in death. Jesus told John to become like a son to Mary, and take care of her. **Family is your greatest investment!** Jesus made sure they were taken care of. He also obeyed the Word that says *"Honor your Father and Mother"*. Jesus showed honor to His earthly mother. The one who raise Him and cared for Him. Honoring your parents is very important to God. A parent is a life source…we must always show honor to those who gave us life both physical and spiritual. That means you should also honor your spiritual parents, mentors, and fathers in the faith. Sow back into them because they gave so much to you. Honor in the New Testament can be translated as a money term in the *greek* text. We should honor the life sources on earth that God put in our lives. Send them gifts and offerings, pay for your parents travels and expenses. Don't always look for something from them, but give something to them and make sure they are taken care of. Jesus did!

6.   "I Am Thirsty" (John 19:28). Of all the sensations that Jesus was feeling on the Cross, the pain, the sin, the weight, the shame, it seems weird that He would even recognize that He was thirsty. Of course Jesus was not talking about physical thirst, there were too many other things going on in His body at that moment. Jesus was telling us that He was Spiritually Thirsty! Having been separated from the presence of God on the cross...this was the only time Jesus ever felt the absence of God. He felt our DEPRAVITY, our inability to know the sweet presence of The Father. He was thirsty for the presence of God. **He became thirsty...so that we could become satisfied!** In fact the Bible says they put vinegar on a sponge and tried to give it to Him and He pushed it away, because He was not talking about physical thirst but spiritual thirst. A life separate from the **living water** of God's presence! Jesus said to the woman at the well... *"But whoever drinks of the water I shall give you, shall never thirst again" (John 4:14).* Jesus didn't tell the woman to not be thirsty, He just told her to switch wells. See, that is what the Church does so often instead of telling the world where to find the water, we just tell them not to be thirsty. That's ridiculous...we're thirsty because God gave us a desire for Him. The world is drinking from the wrong well like this woman; they are trying to quench their thirst with temporary pleasures that simply don't last. We need to let them know where the REAL water is, His name is Jesus! **Jesus**

became thirsty so our thirst could be QUENCHED!

7. "IT IS FINISHED" (John 19:30). Probably the one phrase that struck fear in the heart of the enemy more than any other. In the *greek* this phrase means…**debt discharged.** At this point, Jesus was saying, my task is to complete the debt against humanity so it is charged off! When a debt is charged off it means that you no longer have to pay it. The invoice that you owed God that was more than you could ever pay has stamped at the bottom of it…PAID IN FULL…written in red letters with The Blood of Jesus. If you put your faith in The Son of God, Jesus Christ, you will never have to pay for your sins, Jesus already paid it for you on the Cross. It is finished, over, absolved, forgiven, removed, lifted, and taken away. When someone in the Roman culture had a debt that they couldn't pay against them; the creditor would nail the papers on the doorpost of their house. So everyone who walked by that home saw the debt nailed to the post, and knew how much they owed. Well, Jesus nailed our debt to the post of the cross, and everyone who looks at it sees HIM and not our debt anymore. Hallelujah! Jesus said, "IT IS FINISHED", Pray this prayer with me:

Father, I thank you for your Son Jesus and The Blood that broke every curse and released every blessing over my life. I now apply that Blood to every area of my life. I believe that you are restoring everything that I lost. Jesus come into my heart and take my sins and my mistakes and wash me by your Blood. I give you my life...and I receive Your life NOW! In Jesus Name...Amen!

Is Your Name in The Book?

"...but only those whose names are written in the Lamb's Book of Life." Revelation 21:27

We've made Church about a lot of different things today! We've made Church about growth and technology and trends and fads. We so often forget that Church is important but we are not called to fill up the Church membership roll as much as we are called to fill up Heaven's roll. The Lamb's Book of Life is the document that the Book of Revelation tells us has the names of all the Believers that have accepted Jesus and been born again. There are many on the Church books that have never made it into Heavens BOOK. Don't miss heaven or allow others to miss heaven because you thought going to Church was enough.

The Cross is not a door to Church...The Cross is The door to The Kingdom of God...to relationship with God. Heaven cannot contain or accept anything that is corrupt...impure...or sinful. Your name cannot get in that book because you're good enough. Your name cannot get in that book because you said enough prayers or fed enough children. Your name can only get into that book because you accepted the GIFT of The Cross! We need to get back to the foundation of what the Church is all about...leading people to The Cross not to the Church. Jesus said *"If I be lifted up I will draw all me unto me."* He didn't say if the Church be lifted up or if men of God be lifted up...He said "If I...". **Religion will never get you to heaven...only Jesus can do that.**

This is a big problem in the Body of Christ. We've moved to being satisfied with church attendance rather than people truly being saved. Just because somebody goes to church doesn't mean that they're saved. We must understand this basic fundamental principal in the Kingdom of God. Church is not the door into the Kingdom; Jesus is. Jesus says "I am the door." The only way into the Kingdom of God is through the door of the cross.

So I found myself frustrated as many other believers because we're trying to disciple people, teach them prosperity, teach them blessing, teach them about the Holy Spirit, teach them about the basic principles of the bible, the Christian faith and the Kingdom of God, however we've skipped the most important step. The most important step is have they come through the door of the cross? The greatest day on earth and the greatest moment in history, if you could pick just one, what moment would that be? This is a profound question. Many think the discovery that the earth was round would be one of the greatest moments in history; or the discovery of some particular law of physics; or some other great archeological find would be the greatest discovery or the greatest moment in history.

Well, I believe the greatest moment in history was when the first drop of blood broke through the flesh of Jesus' body because that was the day the door of the kingdom was opened forever, and led to the cross. The cross is the only way into the Kingdom of God. I've titled this book *Confronted by the Cross* because everybody in their life will have to make a decision about the cross. The cross is not a passive decision. The cross is confrontational. When you come through the door of the cross you're introduced to pleasures forevermore in the Kingdom of God, however, we cannot skip the first and most important step. It's a relationship with God; it is understanding the confrontation of the cross.

Am I downing the Church...of course not...Church is a vehicle to lead people to Jesus and The Kingdom of God. It's the Church's Job to teach God's people what's behind that Cross and how they can access all that He paid for. The Bible says clearly, *"He who knew no sin became sin for us all, that we might become the righteousness of God in Christ Jesus."* **He became what you were...so that you could become what He is**...He became SIN so that you could become His righteousness. **He became what He was not (Sin), so that you could become what you were not (Righteous and Holy).** The Bible is also clear on the fact that Jesus became a CURSE. Colossians 3 tells us that *"cursed is the man who hangs on a tree."* Jesus not only broke that curse, He became the curse that was on all of humanity. Jesus said, *"as Moses lifted up the serpent in the wilderness, so must the Son of man be lifted up.(John 3:14)"* You remember the story Jesus was referring to, when the Israelites committed a great sin and snakes began to bite and kill them because their actions had brought a plague on them. God told Moses to make a golden snake and put it on a pole lifted high in the air, and whoever looked at it would LIVE. Jesus was saying, *I am going to be lifted up like that snake;* snakes represent a curse. He was saying I will become the Curse, and whoever looks at me shall LIVE. See we've all been **snake-bit.** Because of Adam we are all like the Israelites, bitten by the snake, and born in iniquity. Nobody had to teach you how to do wrong, you already knew how because it was in your DNA. It was in your blood, because of what Adam did. Jesus became that curse and became that sin, and became that snake on a pole, so you could look and LIVE!

So if Jesus took your curse, took your sin, took your poverty, and took your place that means **He must have given you something in exchange for it.** *God never takes something from you without the intention of giving you back something a whole lot better.* Well, that's exactly what He did. He took your curse and gave you HIS Blessing…He took your sin and gave you HIS righteousness…He took your sickness, and gave you HIS healing…He took your pain and sorrow, and gave you HIS joy and peace. **You see, the cross was simply an exchange**, where Jesus took your bad stuff and gave you His good stuff; He took your death, and gave you His life. So the next time you see a movie or a picture of Jesus on the cross, remember that you are not seeing His humiliation, pain, or shame; you are seeing YOURS. Paid in full, that's right, the blood of Jesus changed your very DNA from sin nature to God nature. **You received a blood transfusion the moment that you believed, and royal blood began to flow in your very veins.** All that shame and pain that you see on Jesus you will never have to feel, because He took your place! This is what the Church should be teaching those that accept what Jesus did on the Cross.

I know that people look like they have it all together…but there are places in their lives that you cannot see; though they look FREE they are really in bondage. Seven is the biblical number of completion, so the seven places of restoration indicate complete restoration. **We can be healed, but not whole.** Wholeness in the Hebrew means, nothing missing nothing broken. Many have been healed by the touch of Jesus, but many are not yet whole because there are still missing areas of restoration that we have not allowed Jesus to deal with. **We can be forgiven but not perfected!** Healed but not HOLY…Delivered but not DISCIPLED.

Ok preacher, you told me about all the bad stuff and all the areas of my life that are fallen, what is the good news? Well, here it goes! **The good news is that Jesus didn't shed His blood one time!** What did you say? Jesus did not shed His blood one time. He shed His blood seven times. If forgiveness of sins was all we needed then why did Jesus shed His blood seven different times and seven different ways. Why didn't the Roman soldiers just stab Jesus in the heart and kill Him? **Because the way He died is just as important as why He died.** If the devil brings seven spirits to control the seven areas of your life then Jesus must have shed His blood seven different ways in order to set you free in those seven areas of your life. Let's see now, how did He shed His blood?

1 – Crown of Thorns – John 19:5

2 – Sweat drops of blood – Luke 22:44

3 – Beard ripped out – Isaiah 50:6

4 – Stripes on His back – John 19:1

5 – Nails in His hands – John 20:27

6 – Pierced His side – John 19:34

7 – Nails in His feet – John 24:40

So what are you trying to say? It is obvious to me that Jesus shed His blood in the same places that represent the seven areas of our life that we need restoration in. Let's put the two lists together and see if they make sense:

Seven areas of our lives **Seven areas Jesus Bled**

1 – Our authority	1 – Crown of thorns
2 – Our mind	2 – Sweat drop of blood
3 – Our communication	3 – Beard ripped out
4 – Our Body	4 – Stripes on His back
5 – Our Prosperity	5 – Nail in Hands
6 – Our relationships	6 – Pierced side
7 – Our Destiny	7 – Nails in His feet

It's kind of like a puzzle. It all goes together if you look at it properly. The seven areas of our lives are the same places that Jesus suffered and bled. You can walk in authority because Jesus bled from the top of His head for you when the crown of thorns was placed on Him. You can have the mind of Christ because Jesus bled from His forehead in the garden like great drops of blood. You can communicate with God again and powerfully with others, because Jesus bled from His mouth when His beard was ripped out. You can be healed in your body because of the stripes that He took on His back for your healing. You can prosper because Jesus bled from His hands when the nails pierced them. So, now the work of your hands can be blessed. You can have godly relationships because Jesus bled from His side, where Adam's bride was pulled from. So now we can walk side by side in Him. Finally, you can fulfill the destiny that God created you for, as well as your eternal destiny, because Jesus bled from His feet when the nail pierced them. **Jesus died a multidimensional death so that you could live a multidimensional LIFE!** When Adam sinned we lost our Position of Authority...We lost our minds...We lost our ability to communicate on a God level...We lost our health...we lost our Prosperity...and we lost our ability for godly relationships...finally, we lost our way back to GOD! Jesus came to give it all back to you! It's all in the Cross!

Pray this Prayer Today!

Father I want to experience all that you provided for me at the Cross. Your forgiveness...Your healing...Your Blessing...Your peace...Your

Word…Your power…Your deliverance…and Your Favor…I receive it now IN Jesus Name Amen!

Now You're Ready!

Wisdom brings Confidence! You now have more than enough information to feel confident that you are able to share your faith without fear and the Holy Spirit has equipped you and Anointed you to be a powerful mouthpiece for The TRUTH. Let's review the steps to confronting someone with the Cross and believe God to empower you to share your faith.

How to confront someone with The Cross:

o The GOD-MOMENT - During conversation with an individual...look for the GOD-MOMENT. The moment when The Holy Spirit nudges you or the window opens that you feel in your heart is a good time for you to Segway into the conversation. This step is crucial because God may already be drawing that person by His Spirit and the timing on your words will confirm what God has already been speaking to them. *Philip was able to recognize when the Holy Spirit was instructing him to confront the Eunuch. When confronting people with the cross you must look for a God opportunity in a conversation or a nudge from The Holy Spirit move the conversation in the direction of the cross.*

o PERMISSION – always Segway with a question. When confronting them with the cross solicit their opinion about God. Ask them what they think about The Cross or the Bible. This step will create permission. Once you listen to their thoughts on the Cross immediately in their mind you create permission to speak to them. This is the law of listening. *Philip asked the eunuch a question..."Do you understand what you're reading?"* Win their permission...*Before you confront them with the Cross ask for their perspective. Ask them what the Cross means to them or if they've ever heard of the Cross. Say things like..."What do you think?" This earns you your right to speak. If you've listened to them...they now will feel obligated to listen to you because you cared enough to get their perspective. Philip asked a questioned..."Do you understand what you're reading?"*

o CONFRONT THEM WITH THE CROSS – now this is your time to shine. Tell them about the Cross about the free gift of forgiveness and salvation. Tell them about the perfect sacrifice of Jesus and how God so loved the world that He gave us His Son. Talk about how the Cross changed your life and how the burden of your sins were lifted. The cross is the greatest moment in history. The cross is not just a historical moment, the cross is a door. It is not a door only, it is THE DOOR to The Kingdom of God...the ONLY DOOR. Jesus said in scripture I AM THE Way, The Truth, and The Life. He didn't say I AM a way...He said I AM THE

WAY. The cross is the door into a new kingdom. The Cross is the place of exchange; your sin for His righteousness, your curse for His Blessing, your shame for His Peace.

o TWO OPTIONS – this is where you share there are only two options. 1. They can accept what Jesus did on the cross and receive everything that he provided through the cross. They can choose to believe and say yes to the cross, and experience **immediate** transformation, immediate restoration in their relationship with God, and immediate access to heaven in eternity. Instantly they will receive everything that the cross provided for them.
2. They can also choose to not believe. They can choose to not accept what Jesus did on the cross, and their life will continue on. They will continue to live life in a way that they see fit without God's involvement and help, only to die and spend eternity in hell. When you're confronted with the cross, those are the only two options you have; to accept the cross or to not accept the cross. Once you make that decision, the consequences have already been set in motion, either access to divine presence and eternal life or a life without God in eternity in

hell. *Don't go into theological details or ideas, just present the two options to either accept the cross or reject it. Here are the results:*

○ DIRECT a decision - The Cross DEMANDS a response...*Philip confronted the Eunuch until he decided to be baptized. Lead in with a question that will direct them to one of the only two choices. You can say things like "So have you accepted Him" or "Would you like to accept what Jesus did now?"*

○ Let the Holy Spirit work...*Realize that once you are finished confronting them with the Cross then the blood is off your hands. You made them aware of the two choices and the results of each choice. Now it's God's turn. Get out of the way and let God do what only He can...Let the Holy Spirit draw and save. You're done with your job.* Let it go...let them go and continue on as if you never did anything. You are not Holy Spirit junior so you don't need to help God out. Jesus saved...we do not. Know at this point that you have obeyed the mandate of heaven that Jesus gave. You have fulfilled the great commission and confronted someone with The Cross. Great job! Now watch God work!

Don't preach at people, make it a conversation and hear their perspective. **Don't react, don't be pushy, and don't judge.** Just wait for that opportunity to present the two options and direct them to a decision. The rest is up to The Holy Spirit. You did your job and only God can save. I challenge you to confront someone with the Cross this week. Look for the God-moments and be ready when the Holy Spirit nudges you. Practice in front of your mirror. You are sharing the greatest message on earth...practice communicating this message with passion and love. Practice with your family by confronting them with the Cross and initiating dialogue about confronting people with the cross.

5 Keys to communicating better:

1. Body language...learn to master the art of non-verbal communication. **People see you before they hear you.** Make them feel listened too just by the way you position your body. By the eye contact you make...by bringing all of you into the conversation. Crossed arms, slouching, and wondering eyes don't connect well with those you're

speaking to. Look into their eyes and lean towards the person you are speaking to letting them know you care about their words.

2. Slow down…**speak to be understood not to be heard.** Most people talk way too fast. Learn to slow down your sentences so that your words can be absorbed and understood.

3. Convey passion…don't speak in a monotone voice. Speak with passion and excitement. Learn to speak words with feeling. Now don't get carried away because they have to be genuine feelings not just flattery. Enunciate your words correctly. **Slurred words and lazy articulation decrease the power of what you're trying to convey.**

4. Ask questions…the most important part of a conversation is a question. Don't give answers…give questions. Because when you give questions…answers show up. Questions take the conversation deeper and keep the conversation going. Learning to ask questions appropriately increases your ability to connect with people and gather information in order to learn about them. **Never enter a conversation as an**

expert...enter as the student even if you know more than the person you are talking too. You make people feel more important when you decide to enter the conversation as a learner. You make yourself look smarter too.

5. Be present...as I stated earlier bring ALL of you into the conversation. Put down cell phones and devices. Focus all your thoughts on what the person is saying. **Become a master listener.** When you do, your words will have more focus and power. When a person knows that you're all in...they feel validated and that what they have to say matters to you. Bring all of you into a conversation and remove distractions that would keep you from being in the moment.

You're on your way to making an incredible impact on the lives of those that you come in contact with on this journey called life. You can't take anything with you to heaven. Not your cars...your house...or your money. You can however take one thing to Heaven with you...and that is the people who you confront with the Cross. People are the only thing you can take through those pearly gates and present to Jesus. Well you better get started!

Pray with me! Father I have learned how to share my faith without fear. Now Anoint me with the power and clarity of The Holy Spirit to recognize the God-moment and have the confidence to confront people everywhere with the Cross. Make me your mouthpiece and use me to impact the lives of those around me. I receive your favor and Anointing to confront people with the Cross...in Jesus Name...Amen!

To Have Bishop Paul Wondracek speak at one of your next events...

Contact the ministry: www.bishopp.tv

Or e-mail us at pastorptv@yahoo.com

Make sure you check out other powerful books from Bishop Paul Wondracek!www.bishopp.tv

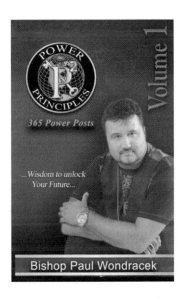